Big Book of
Things
to Make
and Do

PaRragon

Bath · New York · Singapore · Hong Kong · Cologne · Delhi
Melbourne · Amsterdam · Johannesburg · Auckland · Shenzhen

This edition published by Parragon in 2011

Parragon
Queen Street House
4 Queen Street
Bath BA1 1HE, UK

ISBN 978-1-4454-2524-5

Printed in China

Contents

Tips for Success	4		Dazzling Tiaras	52
Precious Purse	6		Pretty Necklace	54
Starry Pen Tube	8		Rose Brooch	56
Musical Tin	10		Castle Jewellery Stand	58
Beautiful Bath Salts	12		Sparkly Star Charm	60
Bird Feeder	14		Ariel Ocean Bracelet	62
Palace Invitations	16		Belle	64
Cinderella	18		Heart Diary	66
Sock Mice Friends	20		Shimmering Fish	68
Shimmer and Shine Frame	22		Pet Photo Frame	70
Petal Tea Set	24		Enchanting Envelopes	72
Water Lily Apron	26		Fabulous Florals	74
Colourful Flower Pot	28		Pressed Flower Card	76
Pretty Paw Prints	30		Bright Room Tidy	77
Beautiful Bird Bath	32		Magical Lamp Holder	78
Snow White	34		Tiana	80
Flower Garland	36		Candy Cushions	82
Flower Candies	38		Bubble Gift Wrap	84
Heart Pillow Case	40		Precious Display Case	86
Rose Magazine Holder	42		Friendship Bracelet	88
Pretty Scented Bags	44		Royal Crown	90
Flutter Butterfly Clips	46		Beautiful Fan	92
Ariel	48		Celebration Mask	94
Shell Jewellery Box	50		Glitter Slippers	96

Tips for Success

Remember, everything in this book should be made with the supervision and help of a grown up! A step labelled with "Kids" means that a child can do this step on their own. Some items will need to purchased from a supermarket or a craft/hobby store.

1 Prepare your space

Cover your workspace with newspaper or a plastic or paper tablecloth. Make sure you are wearing clothes (including shoes!) that you don't mind becoming spattered with food, paint or glue. But relax! You'll never completely avoid mess; in fact, it's part of the fun!

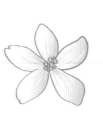

2 Wash your hands

Wash your hands before starting a new project, and clean up as you go along. Clean hands make for clean crafts! Remember to wash your hands afterwards too, using soap and warm water to get off any of the remaining materials.

3 Follow steps carefully

Follow each step carefully, and in the sequence in which it appears. We've tested all the projects; we know they work, and we want them to work for you, too.

4 Measure precisely

If a project gives you measurements, use your ruler, measuring scales, or measuring spoons to make sure you measure as accurately as you can. Sometimes, the success of the project may depend on it.

5 Be patient

You may need to wait while something bakes or leave paint, glue or clay to dry, sometimes for a few hours or even overnight. Be patient! Plan another activity while you wait, but it's important not to rush something as it may affect the outcome!

6 Clean up

When you've finished your project, clean up any mess. Store all the materials together so that they are ready for the next time you want to make and do. If you are making something with someone else then ensure it is a team effort!

Ariel Precious Purse

This precious purse is perfect for keeping your coins and treasures safe. Make one for someone you treasure!

You will need

- Cloth that won't fray
- 20 inches (50cm) cord, ribbon or wool
- 1 large bead
- Large plate and small plate
- Felt tip pen
- Scissors
- Coloured card
- Buttons or beads

Kids

1

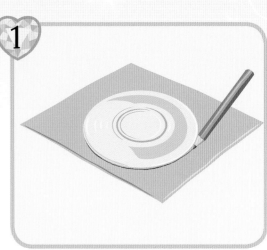

Put the cloth face down. Trace around a large plate onto the wrong side of the cloth. Then cut out the circle. Using a smaller plate, draw another circle on to the cloth in the centre of the bigger circle.

2

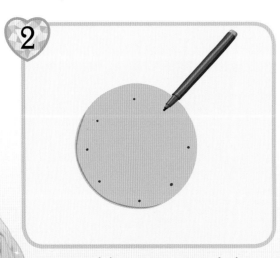

Use a felt tip pen to mark dots at 12, 3, 6 and 9 o'clock around the inner circle. Make dots in between these. Mark 8 more dots in between so that you have 16 dots altogether. Cut a tiny slit on each dot.

3

Draw and cut out a heart shape from coloured card. Decorate the card and make a small hole near the top.

6

4

Cut a piece of cord, ribbon or wool long enough to go around the circle twice. Thread it in and out of the slits, slipping the heart on after the 4th slit.

5

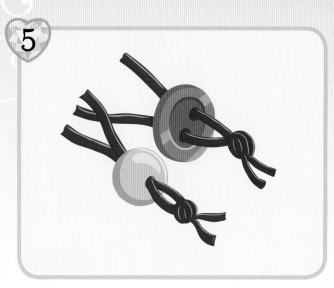

Thread both ends of the cord through a large bead or button and knot the ends together. Now you are ready to decorate your purse and give it to someone special!

Ariel's tip:
Decorate your purse with sequins, beads or stick-on jewels.

7

Starry Pen Tube

Make a tube to hold pens, pencils, or crayons for yourself or give it as a gift. This one is designed like the night sky with stars and comets.

1

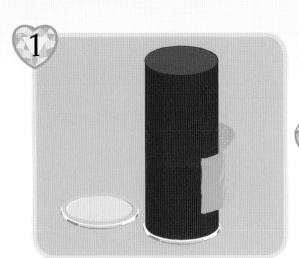

Lightly rub the tube all over with sandpaper. This will help the paint stick better to the tube.

You will need

- Cardboard tube with lid
- Fine sandpaper
- Black acrylic paint
- Paintbrush
- White glue and brush
- Glitter: gold, silver
- Scrap paper
- Sequins and star stickers

Kids

2

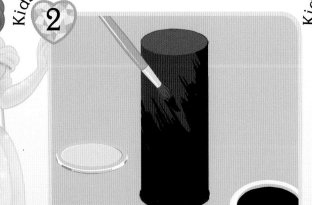

Cover the tube in black acrylic paint. Let dry, then apply another coat. Let the tube dry thoroughly.

Kids

3

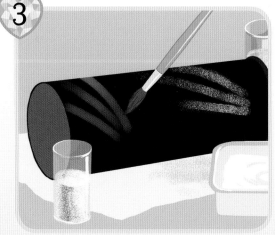

Brush some glue onto the tube then sprinkle the glitter over the top. Shake off the excess glitter onto a piece of scrap paper.

4

Add the star stickers. Glue a row of sequins around the top and bottom of the tube, or anywhere to make your pen tube shimmer.

Belle's tip:
Stars shine brightly at night. This would make a wonderful gift for someone who you think is a super star!

Tiana Musical Tin

Tiana lives in the Bayou, a place full of music! Make this musical themed tin and add some cheer to your room!

1

Cut out three small ovals (approx. ¾ inch (2cm) diameter) and thin strips from craft foam. Stick them onto some thick card into music note shapes. Do this in reverse so the printed design will look correct.

You will need

- A biscuit or cake tin with a lid
- A strip of paper long enough to wrap around a tin
- A paper circle to fit the lid
- Tape
- Craft foam
- Scissors
- Card
- Glue
- Paint
- Brush
- Glitter glue

2

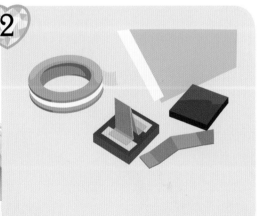

Tape thin strips of folded card onto the top of the printing blocks so they are easy to hold. Tape the strip of paper (for the tin) to your work space.

3

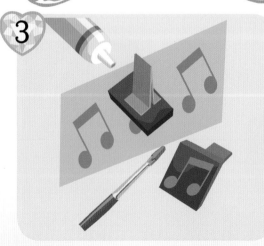

Brush paint over the music notes then press down firmly onto the paper. Re-paint the block after making each print. Add spirals with glitter glue. Leave to dry. Print a design onto a paper circle in the same way for the lid.

4

Wrap the strip around the tin and tape the ends together. Glue the circle to the lid. Put some tasty treats inside. Or use as room storage to keep stationary or jewellery inside.

Tiana's tip:
Now you have a printing block you can use again. Try using it on something else!

Aurora Beautiful Bath Salts

These lovely bath salts add colour to the bathroom and smell sweet every bath time!

You will need

- Small gift jars with tight fitting lids
- Epsom salts – enough to fill the jars
- Food colouring
- Small bowls or plastic containers
- Spoons
- A few drops of essential oil
- Ribbon – 11½ inches (30cm) per jar and a gemstone
- Glue

1

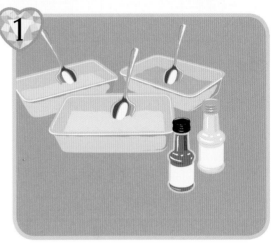

Divide the Epsom salts equally into three plastic containers or bowls. Add a few drops of food colouring and essential oil to each cup. Mix with a spoon. The colours should be quite pale and pretty.

Kids 2

Carefully spoon the first colour into the jars. Press the salt down as you go so it is packed tight. Drop your essential oil onto the top.

Kids 3

Using separate spoons for each colour add the other colours to make a stripy pattern in the jars, adding a few drops of essential oil to each layer.

Put the lids firmly onto the jars. Tie ribbons around the top with a blob of glue to keep it in place. Glue a sparkly gem to the middle.

Aurora's tip:
Make these for your friends in their favourite colours!

Bird Feeder

Snow White loves this bird feeder because she loves to help her bird friends.

You will need

- Empty, rinsed-out juice carton with a nozzle
- Sandpaper
- Scissors
- Acrylic paints
- Paintbrush
- Bird seed
- Garden wire
- Mesh netting bag
- Varnish

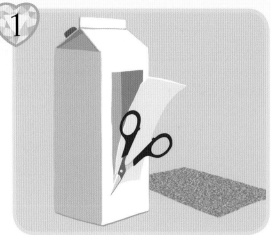

1

Rub the outside of the carton with sandpaper until it's rough. Cut out a rectangular hole on the side facing away from the nozzle.

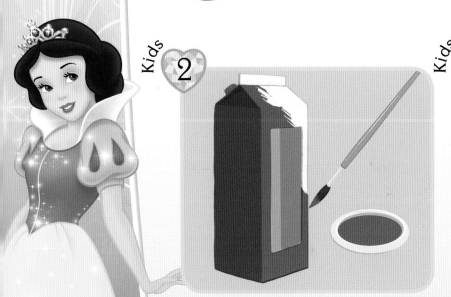

Kids 2

Paint the carton all over in one colour. This one is brown to look like tree bark.

Kids 3

After the paint is dry, add different shades and colours. This one has knots and vines, just like bark.

4

Add leaves or other decorations in a different colour. When you've finished painting, add a coat of varnish to help protect the feeder during cold and wet months.

5

Fill the mesh netting bag with birdseed, then push it through the rectangular hole in the feeder. Remove the nozzle, then pull the top of the bag through the spout. Next, thread wire through the top of the bag and twist the ends together. Hang the feeder up outside.

Snow White's tip:
Hang from a washing line if you don't have a tree in your garden!

Palace Invitations

Whether you're hosting a tea party or a big birthday bash, sending personal handmade invites to your friends is always something special!

You will need

- Coloured card in 2 shades of blue, light and dark
- Paper in gold, silver and purple
- Glue
- Scissors
- Sequins, gems, sequin or sticky stars

1 Cut out a rectangular card shape from the light blue card. Fold in half. Stick a slightly smaller dark blue rectangular card to the front of the larger piece.

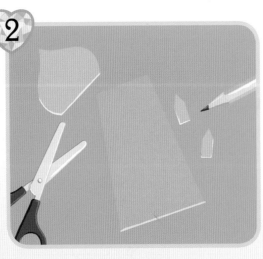

2 To make the palace tower cut out a tall rectangular shape from the purple paper. Then cut out an onion shape from the gold paper to go on top.

3 Stick the shapes onto the background. Leave the glue to dry. Cut out a moon shape from the silver paper.

Add stars and sequins using glue. Glue on your moon. Leave to dry then write your party invitation message on the front or inside of the card.

Jasmine's tip:
You can use glitter and glue to make a starry night sky.

Jasmine's Palace Party

Cinderella

Favourite place:
The ballroom in the castle.

Best friends:
Gus, Jaq and Suzy - her mice friends.

Favourite things:
Beautiful fabrics, a scrapbook, her mother's books and keepsakes.

Best outfit:
Her flowing pale blue gown with matching gloves.

Personality:
She is shy at times but strong-willed, hard-working and determined. Cinderella always likes to see the good in everyone.

The Perfect Gifts

The festive holidays were Cinderella's favourite time of year. She liked to cook holiday treats and make small decorations to put up in the beautiful castle she now called home. Cinderella wanted to give especially wonderful gifts to her mouse friends, who had helped her so much.

First she went to the royal kitchen and asked the cook to make the best cheese pudding for her friends. Then Cinderella went to the royal tailor, and explained that her mouse friends were extra, extra small in size. The tailor helped Cinderella pick out the most beautiful fabrics and assured her that he'd make mouse outfits the likes of which had never been seen. Finally, Cinderella went to the royal carpenter who agreed to make tiny beds, chairs and tables for the mice.

The next day, the cook delivered the delicious pudding, the tailor presented the artfully sewn clothes and the carpenter delivered the tiny furniture which was lovely and elegant. After they left, Cinderella felt something was wrong. She turned to Prince Charming and asked him why she didn't like the gifts … "You know your mouse friends better than anyone else. Maybe you should make their presents." replied the Prince. Cinderella thought that was a wonderful idea and proceeded to make the nicest gifts her mouse friends had ever received.

Turn the page

See what Cinderella made for her mouse friends!

Sock Mice Friends

The mice are Cinderella's bestest friends. Now you can make your own friends cute mice to play with!

Kids

1

Push some cotton wool into a sock so it is around one third full.

You will need

- A small sock
- Scissors
- Wool
- Cotton wool
- Felt
- Fabric glue

2

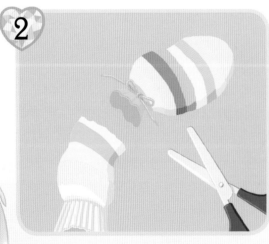

Tie up the end of the sock with a long piece of wool then trim off the open end.

3

Cut two felt circles (approx. 1½ inches (4cm) in diameter). Add glue to one edge of the circles and then pinch the edges together into ear shapes. Leave to dry.

4

Cut small felt circles for the eyes and glue them onto the sock along with the ears and wool whiskers.

Cinderella's tip:

These mice look so cute placed on a pillow when your friends have made their bed!

21

Shimmer & Shine Frame

Make a perfect picture frame from foil and old cardboard. Nobody will ever guess you've been recycling!

You will need

- Thick cardboard 5 x 5 inches (12 x 12cm)
- Thin cardboard 6 x 6 inches (15 x 15cm)
- Ruler
- Scissors
- Tin foil 8 x 8 inches (20 x 20cm)
- White glue and brush
- Old ballpoint pen

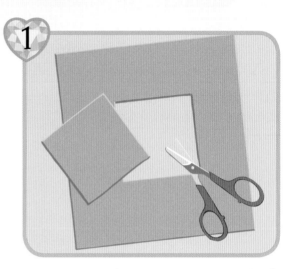

1

Measure and cut out a 2 x 2 inch (5 x 5cm) square hole from the middle of the thick cardboard.

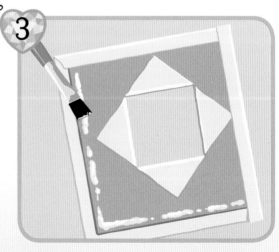

2

Glue the card to the non-shiny side of the foil. Make a hole in the foil and make cuts toward each corner. Fold the triangles you've made onto the back of the frame and glue them down.

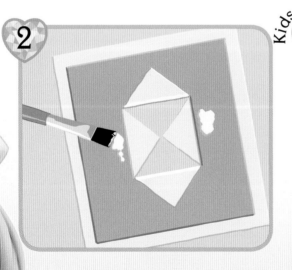

3 Kids

Put a line of glue round the cardboard and glue the four foil edges to it.

22

4

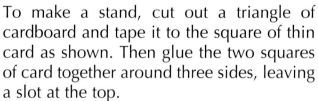

5

To make a stand, cut out a triangle of cardboard and tape it to the square of thin card as shown. Then glue the two squares of card together around three sides, leaving a slot at the top.

Slide a photo into the slot in the frame. Using the empty ballpoint pen, mark your design on the frame. Don't press too hard or you may tear the foil.

Rapunzel's tip:
You could even cut out a heart-shaped frame and decorate it with heart shapes cut from foil candy wrappers.

Petal Tea Set

Every princess loves to host a tea party with their friends. Now you can make your own petal decorated tea set to use over and over again.

You will need

- A plain plate, cup and saucer – washed and dried
- Ceramic paints
- Marker pens
- Small triangle of craft foam taped to the end of a pencil
- Cotton bud or thin felt pen
- Paint brush

Kids 1

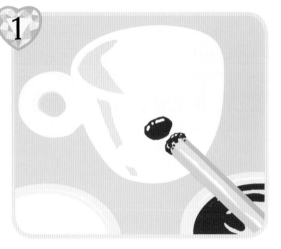

Dip the end of a marker pen into paint and print circles onto the cups and saucers.

2

Cut out leaf shapes into craft foam. These are small triangles. These will be your printing pieces. Dip in green paint and add to your tea set.

Kids 3

When the paint is dry, add smaller dots using the end of a thin pen, cotton bud or paint brush, in the centre of the circles.

4

Belle's tip:
Give someone a lovely
tea party. Pour in apple
juice and pretend
it's tea!

Brush a lighter green onto each leaf shape.
Leave to dry. Then host a tea party!

Tiana
Water Lily Apron

Tiana loves to cook! When you and someone special are baking wonderful treats together you'll both need an apron to protect your clothes.

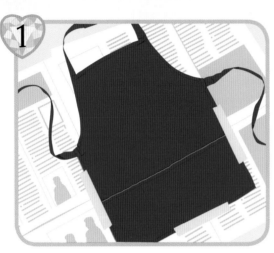

Tape an ironed apron to a table with some card and newspaper underneath.

You will need

- A plain apron
- Masking tape
- A pencil
- Scissors
- Card
- Sponge
- Brushes
- Fabric paints

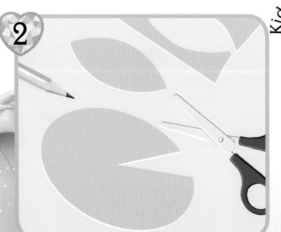

Draw a simple water lily petal shape onto card and also a lily pad shape. Cut them out.

Sponge some white paint onto the petal shaped card, then press it down in the centre of the apron. Repeat this until you have a flower, then leave to dry.

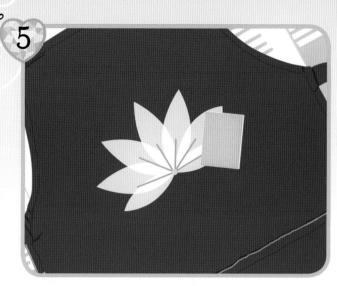

Sponge some pale green paint onto the card lily pad. Print it onto the apron, then flip it over to make another lily pad shape, then leave to dry.

Add a printed pattern to the centre of the flower with a strip of card with paint added to one edge, then paint yellow dots to finish the flower!

Tiana's tip:
As a special touch why not write their name on their new apron!

Aurora

Colourful Flower Pot

Flowers come in all shapes and sizes, and some of them smell so pretty. Make a special pot to keep your favourite bunch of flowers in. Place it in your window and watch your flowers grow!

You will need

- Flower-patterned gift wrap or pictures of flowers from magazines
- White glue and brush
- Plastic flowerpot

Cut out the prettiest flower shapes from the gift wrap or magazines.

Kids **2**

Brush glue around the outside of the plastic flowerpot.

Kids **3**

Glue the cut-out flowers to the flowerpot. Overlap them to make a pretty pattern.

Brush a thin layer of glue over the cut-outs to make the pot waterproof.

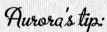

Aurora's tip:
You can decorate some pots with pictures of different leaves, or butterflies, or anything else you like.

Pretty Paw Prints

Your pets deserve the best so make them a wonderful jar to keep their most special treats in!

1

Stick some strips of double-sided tape onto both sheets of coloured card. Cut out eight circles, four pink and four blue from the card.

You will need

- A large empty jar with a lid
- Coloured card – 2 sheets in 2 colours e.g. pink & blue
- Double-sided tape
- Scissors
- Glue and paint brush

2

Kids
3

On the remaining card, draw the paw shapes. Make four blue and four pink. Each paw will consist of a curvy heart shape for the centre and four small ovals. Cut out each paw print.

Glue the paw print patterns onto the card circles. Then peel off the tape from the back of the circles and stick onto the jar. You should have pink on blue and vice versa.

Snow White's tip:
If you don't like paw prints you could try other shapes, such as hearts!

Beautiful Bird Bath

Jasmine loves to watch birds from her bedroom window. Entice pretty birds into your garden with this bird bath and listen to them sing!

You will need

- A plain terracotta pot and base
- Strong glue
- Paint & brushes
- A cork
- A pen or cotton bud
- Leaves

Kids

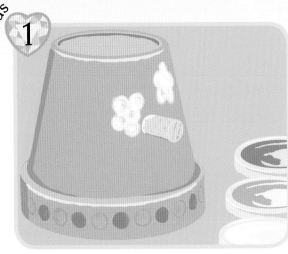

1

Turn the pot upside down. Dip the cork (or thumb print) into white paint and print flower petals onto the pot. Print coloured dots around the edge.

Kids

2

Brush green paint onto the (real) leaves. Press onto the pot to print leaf shapes.

3

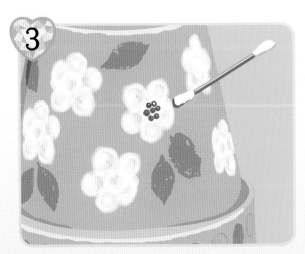

Use a cotton bud to print pink or yellow dots into the middle of the petals. Add a stripe to the middle of the leaves. Leave to dry.

4

Place the saucer on top of the pot and fill the saucer with water.

Jasmine's tip:
Place breadcrumbs around your bird bath!

Snow White

Favourite place:
The little cottage in the woods.

Best friends:
The Seven Dwarfs and forest animals.

Favourite things:
Keeping things tidy and cooking delicious food.

Outfit:
Her yellow skirt with dark blue top, puffed sleeves and tall white collar.

Personality:
Kind-hearted and innocent no matter how horribly her stepmother treats her. She is cheerful and likes to help anyone in need – even the old woman who turns out to be the Evil Queen! Snow White looks after the Seven Dwarfs and keeps their house clean and tidy.

The Prettiest Flower

One morning, Bashful went out to pick the prettiest flower he could find for Snow White's hair. Moments later, he heard a big sneeze – it was Sneezy – he was out picking flowers too. Bashful showed Sneezy his white orchid, and Sneezy showed Bashful his rosebud. They then decided to head home and let Snow White decide which flower she liked best.

On the path back to the cottage, they saw Doc, Happy and Grumpy arguing. Doc had snapdragons. When the Dwarfs arrived at the house, they saw Dopey holding a yellow tulip!

They all went inside the house to greet Snow White, and thank her for being so good to them. Doc asked Snow White to pick the best flower for her hair. Snow White felt terrible – she loved all the Dwarfs and didn't want to hurt any of their feelings by choosing one flower over another. But she had an idea …

She asked the Dwarfs to put all the flowers down on a table and asked them to step outside for a few minutes. When the Dwarfs came back in, they gasped in surprise. Snow White had found a way to wear all their flowers by making a flower crown!

Turn the page

Make Snow White's Flower Garland!

Flower Garland

Make this beautiful flower necklace.
Be inspired by the colours in nature.

You will need

- 80 sheets of tissue paper in 2 different colours (40 of each) cut into squares of 8 x 8 inches (20 x 20cm)
- Bag of pipe cleaners
- Length of elastic or ribbon
- Scissors

Kids **1**

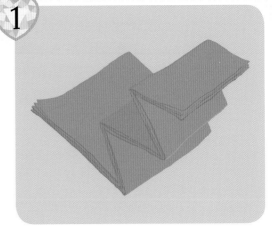

Stack 4 sheets of one colour tissue paper together and fold over 5 times to make an accordian shape.

2

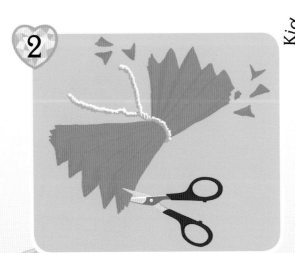

Cut both ends into a round shape then twist a pipe cleaner around the middle. Don't trim the ends of the pipe cleaner.

Kids **3**

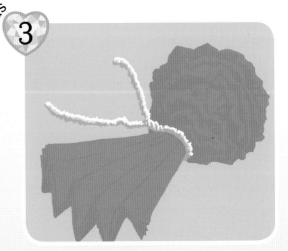

Gently separate out the tissue paper on both sides of the pipe cleaner into a flower shape.

Twist the ends of the pipe cleaner around the ribbon or elastic and make sure the ends are not sticking out. Keep adding flowers until your garland is done.

Snow White's tip:
What's your favourite flower? Use this as inspiration for your garland!

Tiana Flower Candies

Tiana loves to make scrumptious treats for all her friends. You might need a helping hand to make them, but certainly not eating them. Delicious!

You will need

To make 20 candies:
- 8oz (225g) icing sugar
- 1 egg white
- Juice of half a lemon
- A few drops of peppermint extract
- Green food colouring
- Bar of chocolate
- Sieve, bowl, biscuit cutter, wooden spoon, saucepan

Kids

1

Sift the icing sugar into a large mixing bowl.

2

Separate the egg yolk from the white. Add the egg white to the icing sugar.

3

With your hands or a spoon, mix it together until you have made a soft lump. Add the lemon juice, peppermint extract and food colouring.

4

Pour the lump onto a cold surface and flatten it to about ½ inch (1.5cm) thick. With a biscuit cutter, cut out the shapes, put them on a baking sheet, and leave them in a cool, dry place to set for around 30 minutes.

5

Break up the bar of chocolate and put it in a bowl. Put the bowl over a saucepan of simmering water and stir the chocolate until it has melted.

Tiana's tip:

You could make fruit chocs instead. Dip strawberries, cherries and sliced apple in the melted chocolate.

Kids

6

Take the bowl off the heat and quickly dip half of each candy into the chocolate. Leave the candies until the chocolate hardens.

Heart Pillow Case

Aurora's royal bed spreads are covered in beautiful hearts. Sleep like a princess with this pillow case!

1

Push a piece of card inside the pillowcase. Tape the edges to a covered work surface. Place a cut-out card heart in the middle of the pillow case to use as a guide for printing.

You will need

- A plain white pillowcase
- Heart shape cut from card
- A pencil
- A cork
- A felt pen
- Fabric paint
- Saucer

Kids **2**

Pour a small amount of fabric paint into a saucer. Dip a cork into the paint. Use it to print dots around the card heart shape. Dip the cork back into the paint after every two or three dots.

Kids **3**

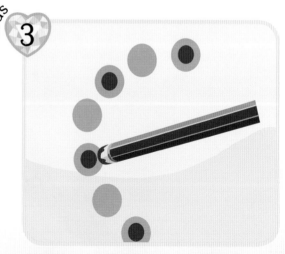

Use the end of a pen dipped into another colour to print smaller dots inside the bigger dots.

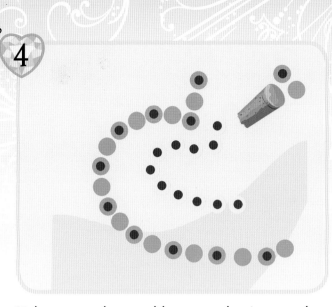

Aurora's tip:
Hearts are only one shape you can try. Why not come up with a starry print design?

Take away the card heart and print another smaller heart shape using different colours inside the bigger heart. Leave to dry thoroughly, then put a pillow inside the case. Sweet dreams.

Rose Magazine Holder

As you know, Belle loves to read. To keep your books or magazines tidy in your room, make this rose inspired holder!

1

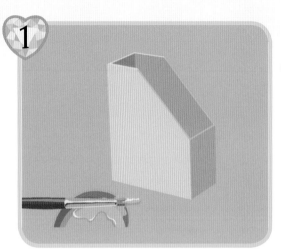

Paint the box all over in a cream colour. Leave to dry.

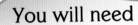

You will need

- A plain file box – or a grocery box cut to the same shape
- Scissors
- Glue
- Paints
- Brushes
- Tissue paper
- A piece of rectangular sponge

2

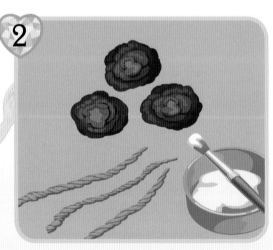

Tear some strips of tissue paper 20 x 4 inches (50 x 10cm). Twist the strips round into a spiral for the roses then brush glue onto the end so the tissue paper doesn't unwind. Twist some green tissue strips for the stems.

3

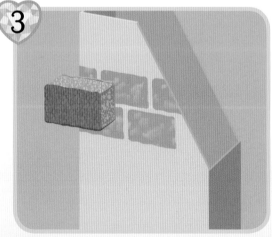

Use a piece of rectangular sponge to print a brick pattern onto the box. Leave to dry.

Belle's tip:
What's your favourite flower? Make this holder with a different flower!

4

Lay the box flat on your worksurface, then stick the stems and flowers onto the sides. (this is easier than doing it standing up). Add some cut out tissue paper leaves.

Pretty Scented Bags

This pretty scented bag is filled with sweet smells! If you place it in your drawer, it will keep your clothes smelling sweet like flowers.

You will need

- Tray
- Lavender flowers
- Rose petals
- Thin fabric 4 x 12 inches (10 x 30cm)
- Fabric glue
- Rubber band
- Coloured ribbon
- Scissors
- Coloured felt or fabric scraps
- Beads or sequins (optional)

Kids 1

Spread out the lavender flowers and rose petals on a tray and allow them to dry for a couple of weeks.

Kids 2

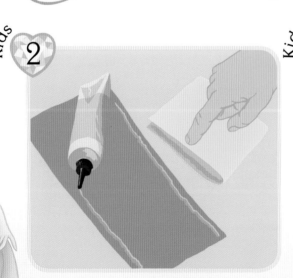

Glue along the long sides of the fabric. Fold in half to make a bag. Press the edges together. Let dry.

Kids 3

Place some of the dried flowers inside the bag and gather the top together with a rubber band, then tie the ribbon on top.

Cut out small shapes from fabric or felt and glue them onto the bag. Glue on beads or sequins for extra decoration.

Cinderella's tip:
Place these bags in your clothes drawer or under your pillow!

Flutter Butterfly Clips

Rapunzel has beautiful long, flowing locks. Create these nature inspired butterfly hair clips and see them flutter and sparkle in your hair!

1

Fold a piece of 4¾ x 4 inches (12 x 10cm) paper in half. Draw half a butterfly shape along the fold, then cut it out.

You will need

- Card
- Coloured paper
- Pencil
- Glitter
- Glue
- Sequins
- Pipe cleaner
- A plain hair clip

2

Thinly brush glue over the butterfly. Don't use too much or it will curl up. Sprinkle different colours of glitter over the glue.

3

Bend a piece of pipe cleaner down the middle of the butterfly for the body. Twist the ends together around the back.

4

Rapunzel's tip:
Another idea you could
try is decorating a hair band.
Try one butterfly on the side
or stick a few across
the top!

Glue sequins for the eyes and spots,
add thin strips of coloured paper for the
antennae. Glue the finished butterfly onto
a plain hair clip. Leave to dry.

Ariel

Favourite place:
The beautiful castle she shares with Prince Eric.

Best friends:
Flounder and Sebastian.

Favourite things:
Music and singing.

Best outfit:
Pink flowing gown with tiara.

Personality:
Sweet and innocent, Ariel is the youngest of King Triton's seven daughters. Her curiosity and adventurous spirit lead her to find out more about the human world, where she falls in love with Prince Eric.

The Wrong Gift

Ariel's sister, Aquata, was celebrating her birthday and friends from across the ocean gathered at her party. Ariel couldn't decide what to give her sister. She and Flounder swam to a secret cave where they looked over a vast collection of bells, clocks, jewellery and knick knacks.

Suddenly Ariel noticed a music box. It was the perfect gift! Ariel swam back to the celebrations, whereupon she saw her father King Triton sitting beside her sister, Aquata. Lining up one-by-one were the guests each presenting their birthday presents.

While Ariel waited in line for her turn, Sebastian swam by and asked Ariel what her gift was. His jaw nearly dropped to the ocean floor when Ariel told him she had a music box. King Triton disliked humans. Arial was not supposed to have anything from the human world – which is why she kept her cave a secret!

Moments later, it was Ariel's turn to present her birthday gift. She hid the music box behind her back, as King Triton asked Ariel to come forward. Ariel couldn't think of what else she could have for her sister - then Sebastian announced that Ariel was to sing a song! But what song? In a flash, Ariel opened her mouth and sang the melody from the music box. When Ariel had finished, Flounder swam behind her and replaced the music box with a beautiful starfish for Aquata's hair.

Turn the page

to make Ariel's shell jewellery box and other glitzy things!

Shell Jewellery Box

Ariel keeps her most precious things safe inside a shell box. These make for wonderful gift boxes or as a present on their own.

You will need

- Round food container with lid
- 2 squares of red felt
- Pencil
- Scissors
- White glue and brush
- Blue acrylic paint and brush
- Assorted seashells

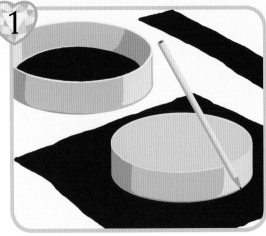

1

Draw around the lid of the box onto the red felt. Cut it out, and stick it inside the lid. Repeat, and stick onto the base of the box.

2

Measure the depth of the box and cut a long strip of felt the same width. Glue it around the inside of the box. Trim the ends to make it fit neatly. Let dry.

3

Paint the outside and base of both the lid and box with the blue acrylic paint.

4

Arrange the shells on the box lid and glue them on.

5

Smaller boxes can be decorated with a single shell. Use them as gift boxes for earrings and rings.

Ariel's tip:
Seashells are the homes of creatures called shellfish. Once the animal has gone, you can use the shells for all sorts of crafts.

Dazzling Tiaras

To dazzle like a princess you need a wonderful tiara to wear. Follow these steps and create a colourful piece of headware.

You will need

- Card
- Cup
- PVA glue
- Tissue paper
- Curly parcel string or ribbon
- Sweet wrappers
- Pipe cleaners or string
- Sticky tape
- Scissors

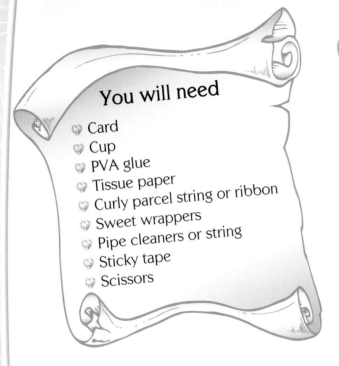

1

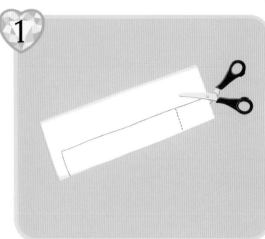

Cut a band of card 1 inch (3cm) wide and long enough to fit around your head with 1½ inches (4cm) overlap at the back. Leave flat. Paint the headband with glue and cover with a layer of tissue paper.

2

Leave it to dry. Then trim the edges with scissors to make it neat. Tape the parcel string or ribbon to the back of the headband at an angle. Wrap it around the headband and tape it at the other end.

3

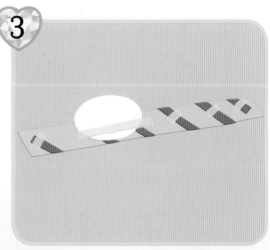

Trace a small circle around a cup onto card. Cut it out. Paint it with glue. Cover it with tissue paper and leave it to dry. Trim the edges to make it neat.

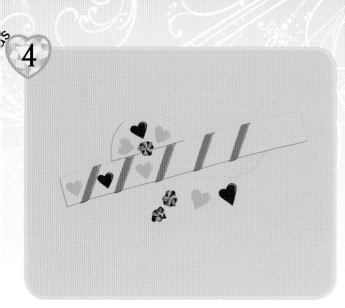

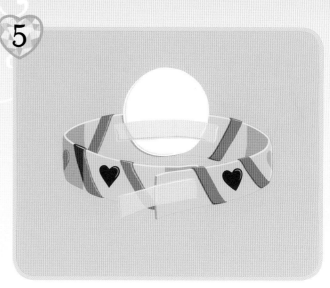

4 Tape the circle face down on the centre back of the headband so that half the circle shows from the front. Now you are ready to decorate your tiara with gold hearts and a scrunched up sweet wrapper.

5 Ask someone to help you hold the band in place around your head and tape it together at the right size. Then take it off and tape the ends.

Rapunzel's tip:
Here are some ideas for other tiaras you could try making.

Tiana Pretty Necklace

Now let's make pasta jewellery with Tiana. You can use these shapes and colours, or choose your own.

Kids

1

Paint the macaroni in a pink princess colour and leave to dry on top of toothpicks stuck into modelling clay. If you want, as an added option, you can add a coating of glue and glitter and leave to dry.

You will need

- Dried pasta shapes: 30 macaroni
- Acrylic paints: pastel pink Glitter and glue
- Lump of modelling clay
- Toothpicks
- Coloured string, elastic, or cord
- Button

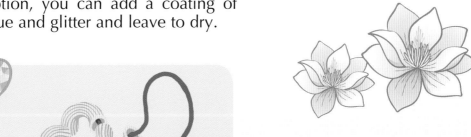

2

Thread each macaroni onto the coloured string or cord. Repeat this until all the pasta is threaded.

Tie a button to the string while you thread the shapes to keep them from falling off!

54

Knot the two ends of the string together, making sure you have made your necklace big enough to go over your head.

Tiana's tip:
There are a lot of different pasta shapes, like twirls or bow ties. Try a different style like in the picture!

Belle Rose Brooch

Roses are very important to Belle. Breaking the spell on the enchanted rose meant that Belle could be with the Prince!

You will need

- A section cut from an egg carton
- Green paint
- Paintbrush
- Red felt 20 x 20 inches (50 x 50cm)
- Scissors
- Glue and tape
- A safety pin

1 Cut off a single section from an egg carton. Cut the sides into points then paint it green to look like the bottom of a rose bud. Leave to dry.

2 Cut out ten circles from your red felt. These should have a diameter of 2¾ inches (7cm).

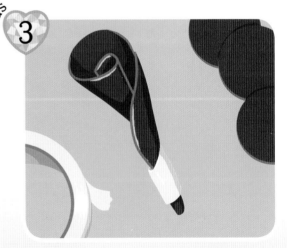

3 Roll up one of the felt circles. Stick some tape around one end. The felt should remain rolled up, but one end should be loose, forming the centre of your rose.

4

Glue the remaining felt circles around this middle piece to form your rose. These should start out quite tight until the outer circles are simply stuck on. Tape a safety pin to the egg carton, then glue the rose inside.

Belle's tip:
You can pin this rose to a top, a coat or even your bag. Beautiful!

Castle Jewellery Stand

A castle is not just a castle, it is also a wonderful way to display your Princess fashion crafts and jewellery!

You will need

- A small cardboard box
- Cardboard tubes – different sizes
- A circular lid – for a balcony
- Coloured card (dark blue) for doors and windows
- Pencil
- Scissors
- Glue
- Masking tape
- Small saucers
- Paints
- Brushes
- Sequins/gems

1 Arrange the tubes around a small box into a good castle shape. Cut the tubes if you need to so they vary in height. Don't glue them together yet.

2 Cut out some circles from card to make the turrets, they need to be around 14cm diameter for smaller turrets and 20 cm diameter for the bigger ones. Cut the circles in half so you have semi circles.

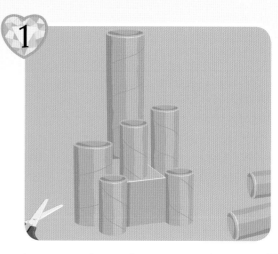

3 Curl the semi circles into cone shapes and stick masking tape along the edge. Place each cone upside down into a small jar (to stop it rolling around) then glue the tube inside it.

4

Glue the turrets together around the box. To make a balcony, glue a lid to the largest turret, then stick the small turret on top. Leave the glue to dry, then paint your castle in a beige colour to make it look like a castle wall.

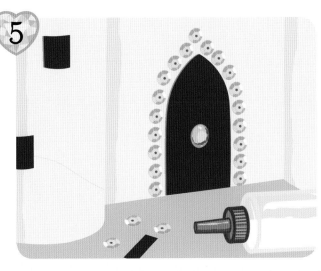

5

When the paint has dried, glue the small windows and a door in place that you have cut out from the card. Glue sequins for extra sparkle. Then display your most precious jewellery from the turrets.

Snow White's tip:
Put this castle somewhere prominent in your room. This castle really needs to be seen!

Sparkly Star Charm

Cinderella loves the sparkle of a night sky filled with stars. Make this star charm and add some sparkle to your wardrobe.

You will need

- Salt dough recipe:

  2 cups (200g) plain flour
  1 cup (200g) of salt
  1 cup (200ml) of water
  1 tablespoon of cooking oil

- A rolling pin
- Star shaped cookie cutters
- A cocktail stick
- Paint
- Brush
- Glue
- Gems
- A key chain or charm chain with a big jump ring

Kids

1

Mix up 2 cups (200g) of plain flour and 1 cup (200g) of salt in a mixing bowl. Add 1 cup (200ml) of water, and 1 tablespoon oil. Mix together into a smooth dough. If your dough is too sticky, add more flour, if it is too crumbly add more water.

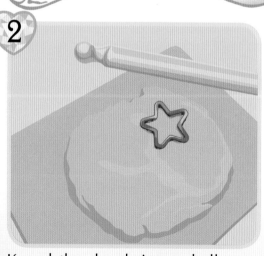

2

Knead the dough into a ball on a floured work surface. Roll it out to ½ inch (1cm) thick. Cut out shapes using small cookie cutters.

3

Make a hole in the top of each shape with a cocktail stick or pencil. Be sure it goes all the way through and doesn't close up. Leave to dry. It could take a few days normally or only a few hours in an oven on a very low temperature.

4

Paint the shapes and leave to dry then glue on gems and glitter. Fix a jump ring through the holes and then attach onto a key chain.

Cinderella's tip:
You could make a heart charm, just cut out heart shapes instead of stars!

Ariel *Ocean Bracelet*

Ariel is always so inspired by the ocean world. These beads are beautiful ocean blues, green and yellows!

1

Roll the three colours of clay into sausage shapes and put them side by side. Using a plastic knife, cut sections of about the same size through all three lengths together.

You will need

- Air–drying clay: green, yellow, turquoise
- Plastic knife
- 15 toothpicks
- Mug or glass
- Darning needle
- Thin elastic thread
- Scissors

Kids

2

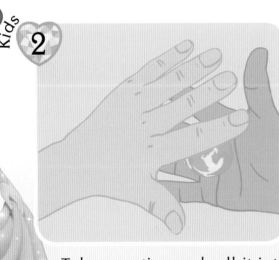

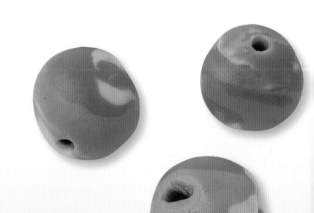

Take a section and roll it into a ball between your palms until the colours are mixed together. Repeat until you have made about 15 balls.

3

Push a toothpick through the middle of each ball. Balance the sticks across the top of a mug or glass, so that the beads are fully exposed to the air, and leave them to dry. They will be ready in about 24 hours.

4

Using a darning needle, thread the beads onto thin elastic until you have enough to go around your wrist comfortably. Knot the two ends of elastic together and trim the ends.

Ariel's tip:
The ocean shimmers with all the colours of the rainbow, so you can make these beads in any colour you like!

Belle

Favourite place:
The castle library.

Best friends:
Cogsworth, Lumiere and Mrs Potts.

Favourite things:
Reading books,
writing in her diary.

Best outfit:
Adores her off-the-shoulder,
golden ball gown and matching
gloves.

Personality:
Belle loves to daydream and has a good imagination. She can be
outspoken and determined especially when refusing to marry
Gaston! Belle is patient and has a caring nature toward others – no
wonder the Beast loves her.

The Mysterious Book

Belle was sitting in the Beast's library daydreaming. Chip noticed Belle staring and asked her what she was looking at. Belle pointed to the highest shelf in the library. On the shelf, there was a single book. Belle had wondered about the book since the first day she was shown the library. The trouble was, none of the ladders quite reached the shelf. So the book had remained a mystery.

Belle's curiosity about the book grew and grew. What could it be about? Surely it had to be the most magical, unusual, wonderful book in the world! Belle couldn't stop thinking about the book and explained the problem to Chip. Chip went and told his mother, Mrs Potts, and she then called a meeting with all the enchanted objects to see how they could help Belle.

They hatched a plan to gather in the library that evening. The Wardrobe stood at the base of the shelves, then the Stove climbed on top of her, then the Coatrack climbed up next. Soon a tower of enchanted objects stretched almost to the top shelf. Finally, Lumiere started to climb, and as he reached out for the book, Belle entered the room. Startled, Lumiere knocked the book off the shelf and it landed into Belle's hands.

Belle couldn't wait to see what wonders lay within the book covers. She settled down with the enchanted objects. Belle turned the cover and saw the first page. "Oh! I can't believe it! I've already read this one!" she smiled sheepishly.

Turn the page

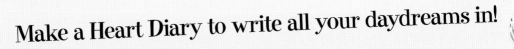

Make a Heart Diary to write all your daydreams in!

Belle | *Heart Diary*

Belle keeps all her most precious secrets and ideas in a diary and writes in it every day. A hand decorated diary makes for a very special present.

Kids

1

Place a piece of paper inside the front and back cover of the notebook, to stop the pages getting paint on them. Cover the notebook with paint, then let it dry.

You will need

- A small plain hardback notebook or diary
- 2 sheets of plain paper
  - if you need to paint the notebook
- Paint – if you need to paint the notebook
- Brushes
- Gold card
- Gemstone
- String
- Glue - PVA in a bottle with nozzle
- Ribbon

2

Cut four triangles of gold card and glue them to the corners of the notebook. Cut a heart shape from gold card and stick in the centre of the cover.

Kids

3

Glue a gemstone in the middle. Glue a curly pattern with glue then stick the string down over the top. Press it down. Add red felt strips around the spine of the book.

Belle's tip:
This would make a wonderful present for your mummy, grandma or best friend!

Stick a ribbon to the inside back cover at the top of the page. This can be used as a bookmark. Now write inside your diary about your day, favourite things and pretty fashion ideas!

Ariel

Shimmering Fish

These fabulous fish are pretty and shimmer just like they do under the ocean. Give some to a friend so they can put them up in a window and watch them shine!

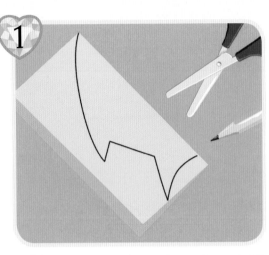

1 Fold a piece of card 15½ x 11½ inches (40 x 30cm) in half. Draw half a fish shape then cut it out so you have a fish shaped template.

You will need

- Card (cut from a cereal box)
- Pencil
- Scissors
- Kitchen foil
- Coloured sweet wrappers and foil
- Glue
- Brush
- White card
- Felt pen
- Thread and tape to hang up

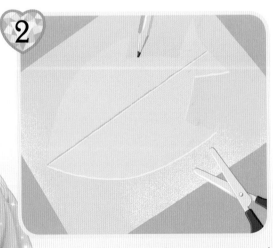

2 Place the template onto card and draw around the edge. Cut it out. You can use the template to make more fish shapes.

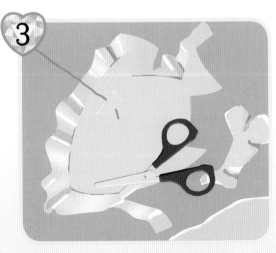

3 Cut two pieces of foil roughly the same size as the fish. Crinkle the foil a bit then paste onto both sides. Press over the foil to stick it down, then trim around the edges.

4

Ariel's tip:

Ariel's tip:
It's fun to make these fish with a best friend and make one for each other!

Glue coloured wrappers/foil onto both sides then trim any overhanging pieces from around the edges. Glue a white card circle onto both sides for the eye. Make a black dot with felt pen. Tape some thread to the top to hang the fish up.

Jasmine Pet Photo Frame

If you know someone who likes animals as much as Jasmine does, then make this cute frame for your friends or family to show off their favourite pet or animal.

You will need

- 4 cardboard strips 6 x 1 inches (15.5 x 2.5cm)
- 12 sticks (same size)
- Cardboard (to fit photo)
- 2 different-sized pens (any kind)
- Acrylic paints
- Scissors
- Clear adhesive tape

Kids 1

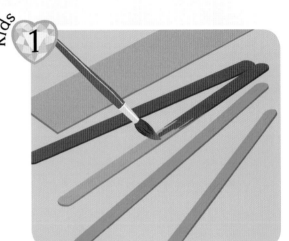

Paint the sticks and let dry (or use coloured ones).

2

Glue three sticks onto each cardboard strip, leaving about an inch (2.5cm) gap at both ends. Then glue the ends of the cardboard strips together into a frame shape.

Kids 3

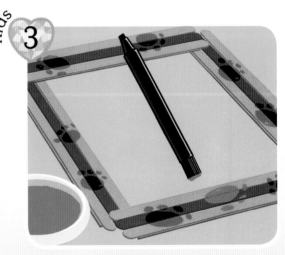

Dip the end of the largest pen into the paint and press down around the frame. Then use the smaller pen to add circles to complete the paw prints.

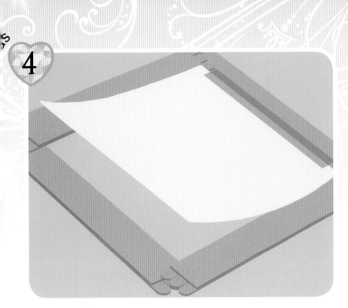

Tape a photo of your pet into the frame then cover the back with a piece of cardboard.

Belle

Enchanting Envelopes

These beautiful princess-inspired envelopes are perfect for sending your party invites. Or for sending your best friend a letter!

You will need

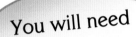

- Sheet of 8½ x 11 inch (21 x 28cm) coloured paper
- Scissors
- Patterned gift wrap
- Glue stick
- A card sized template

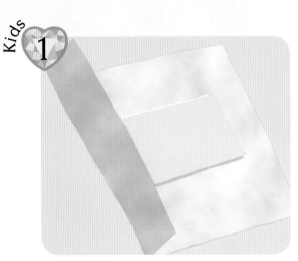

Kids

1

Put your card template on the sheet of coloured paper. Fold the paper in on two sides and the bottom. Then fold over the top of the paper to make the flap.

2

Unfold the paper and cut out the four small corner rectangles.

3

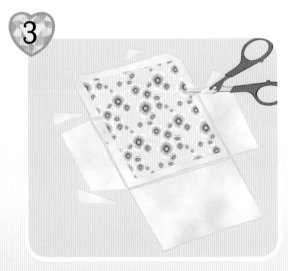

Cut a piece of gift wrap to fit in the top flap and main area. Leave ½ inch (1.5cm) gap around the edge of the gift wrap. Glue in place. Trim the corners of the top and side flaps.

Fold up the bottom flap, then fold in the sides and glue them in place. Place the homemade card inside, then fold down and glue the top flap.

You can make a colourful envelope from patterned paper. Don't forget to add a label with the name of the person you're giving the card to on the front.

Belle's tip:
You can also add colourful stickers to decorate your envelope or to seal them!

Fabulous Florals

Rapunzel has so much fun exploring the forests and smelling sweet flowers. When she needs somewhere to display her flowers, she makes this wonderful vase!

You will need

- A clear vase
- String
- Pebbles
- Marbles
- Beads
- Sparkly gems

Kids 1

Carefully place some rocks inside the vase to cover the bottom.

2

Tie the flowers together with a piece of string and place them into the vase. Push the stems between the rocks so they stand up.

Kids 3

Add some more rocks, marbles and gems around the flowers until the vase is nearly full.

4

Use a jug or watering can to fill the vase with water. It will be very heavy so ask someone to lift it for you. It will look good near a window where the light can shine through.

Rapunzel's tip:
You can use plastic flowers for a permanent allergy free display!

Aurora Pressed-flower Card

Pressed flowers can be used to make beautiful greeting cards. Don't forget to check with an adult before you pick flowers!

You will need

- Flowers and leaves
- Heavy books (e.g. dictionaries)
- Paper towels
- White glue mixed with equal amount of water, and brush
- Cream cardboard 16 x 18 inches (40 x 46cm)
- Scissors and ruler

Kids 1

Pick some flower petals and leaves. Arrange them on paper towels, then put another piece of paper towel on top. Place them inside a book. Place a pile of heavy books on top of the book with the flower, petals, and leaves inside. Leave them for at least two weeks.

Kids 2

Fold the cream cardboard in half and make a sharp crease with the point of the scissors and a ruler. Be careful not to cut the cardboard. Remove the pressed petals and leaves from the book. Arrange them on the front of the card and glue them in position.

Bright Room Tidy

Wastepaper baskets can be beautiful. Cover yours in some brightly coloured gift wrap. There's no need to hide your basket anymore!

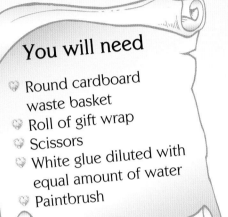

You will need

- Round cardboard waste basket
- Roll of gift wrap
- Scissors
- White glue diluted with equal amount of water
- Paintbrush

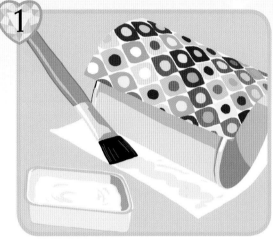

1

Choose gift wrap that you like. Cut a piece a bit larger than the container. Wrap the paper around the container and glue it in place.

2

Make small snips in the top and bottom edges, fold them over and glue them down.

Cinderella's tip:
Ask a grown up about recycling the paper once you've filled your basket.

Magical Lamp Holder

This magical holder is perfect for your bedside. Jasmine keeps her jewellery inside hers. What will you keep inside yours? Will a genie appear?

You will need

- Air drying clay
- Plastic knife
- Rolling pin
- Talcum powder
- A small bowl
- Some water in a bowl
- Pencil
- Paint
- Brush
- Gemstones

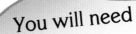

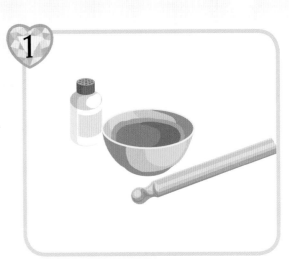

Roll out some clay to about ½ inch (15mm) thick and cut a circle shape 6 inches (15cm) diameter. Shake some talcum powder inside a small bowl then press the clay into the bowl.

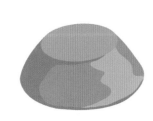

Carefully release the clay, using a plastic knife if you need to (the talcum powder should help make it easier). Turn the clay shape over to flatten the top.

Roll a coil of clay for the handle. Smooth it down on one side of the lamp. Cut a triangular spout from rolled out clay and press a coil to the base. Use a pencil to make dot patterns and a hole in the spout.

4

Turn the lamp over and leave it to dry out. Support the spout with some rolled up paper whilst it is drying.

5

Paint and glue gems around the sides and leave to dry. Add your treasures!

Jasmine's tip:
Your lamp doesn't have to be gold. Paint it in any colour you like!

Tiana

Favourite place:
Her restaurant 'Tiana's Palace'.

Best friends:
Charlotte LaBouff, Louis and Ray.

Favourite things:
cooking delicious food.

Best outfit:
Pale blue ball gown from
La Bouff Masquerade Ball.

Personality:
Strong-willed, independent,
and determined to achieve
her dreams. Although she
wants to do everything her
way, she has a lot to learn.

Tiana's Busy Day

One day, Charlotte rushed into the restaurant calling to Tiana for help. She was holding a ball that night and needed 100 beignets for all the guests! Tiana smiled and calmly went straight into the kitchen. She worked hard all afternoon, and before long, she had a mountain of delicious beignets ready. 'How can I ever thank you?' Charlotte exclaimed, and gave Tiana a big hug before running out the door with the treats.

Just as Tiana was looking forward to a nice rest, her pal Louis came rushing through the door shivering with cold.

'It's a cold day!' he said to Tiana. 'I'm looking forward to some of your home-made stew to warm me up!'

Although Tiana was tired, she didn't want to let her friend down, and she set to work cooking up a delicious, steaming stew for Louis.

By this time Tiana was exhausted, and went home for a quiet rest. Prince Naveen, who had been watching Tiana work so hard, had an idea…When Tiana returned to the restaurant that evening, she couldn't believe her eyes! All her friends were gathered together, and in the centre was an enormous feast! 'You work so hard, we wanted to thank you, Tiana!' Prince Naveen smiled at his princess. 'We cooked all your favorite food, for you and everyone!'

Everyone enjoyed the wonderful food, all the way into the night!

Turn the page

Treat yourself with Tiana's candy cushions!

Tiana Candy Cushions

These comfy, candy-shaped cushions look good enough to eat, a bit like Tiana's beignets! Make a pile and turn your bedroom into a candy shop!

1

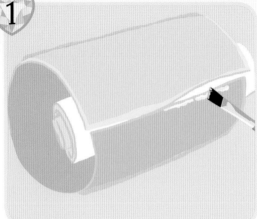

Glue the two pieces of fabric together, one on top of the other, along the longer edges. Glue the short edges together to make a tube. Put newspaper inside to stop the glued seam from sticking to the other side.

You will need

- For each cushion:
- 1 piece of gold-coloured fabric and 1 piece of coloured netting both 20 x 28 inches (30 x 70cm)
- Newspaper
- White glue and brush
- 2 strong rubber bands
- Cushion filling, such as polyester filling
- ½ yard (45cm) gold ribbon

2

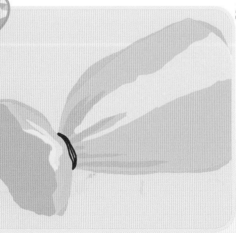

Once dry, gather up one end about 5 inches (13cm) from the edge and hold it in place with one of the rubber bands.

3

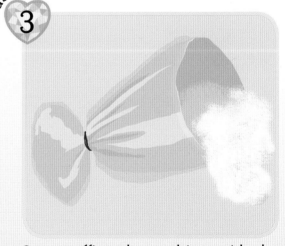

Start stuffing the cushion with the filling until it is filled to about 5 inches (13cm) from the top.

Close the end with the other rubber band. Fan out the ends of the cushion to make them look like candy wrappers.

Glue some gold ribbon over the rubber bands so they don't show.

Tiana's tip:
Recycle old cushions by picking apart the seams and reusing the filling for your groovy new cushions.

Cinderella Bubble Gift Wrap

Now it's time to make some bubbly gift wrap with Cinderella. It's so much fun! Why don't you give it a try?

You will need

- Old newspapers
- Acrylic paints: purple, yellow
- Dish washing liquid
- Water
- Old spoon
- Drinking straws
- Shallow bowl
- White paper
- Measuring spoons

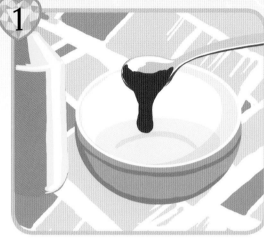

1 Cover your work surface with newspaper. Using a spoon, stir together ¼ pint (120ml) of water, 1 or 2 tablespoons purple paint, and ½ tablespoon dish washing liquid in the bowl.

Kids 2 Place a straw in the paint mixture and gently blow to make bubbles. Keep blowing until the bubbles are almost at the edge of the dish.

Kids 3 Put a piece of paper on top of the bubbles and hold it there until several bubbles have popped. Move the paper and continue popping bubbles until most of the paper has been coloured. Don't push the paper too far into the bowl.

4

Cinderella's tip:
Use a drop more dish washing liquid if you want to make more bubbles.

Clean the bowl and make a yellow paint mixture. Repeat steps 1 to 3 so you have a purple and yellow bubbly pattern on the piece of paper. Let dry before using the paper. Try different colours next time!

Ariel Precious Display Case

Ariel has many trinkets and treasures from the ocean. To present them and keep them safe she has made her own display case. Make your own, it's easy and looks very special!

1

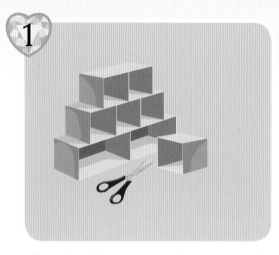

Glue the boxes together. Trim the edges first if they need to be made smaller. Leave to dry.

You will need

- Some small boxes
- Glue
- Paints
- Brush
- Glitter

Kids 2

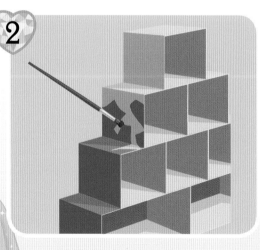

Paint inside the boxes. Make sure your brush reaches into the corners.

Kids 3

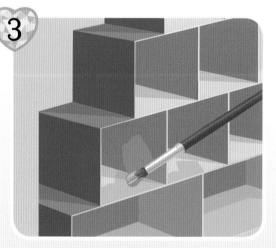

Paint the outside using a different colour. Leave to dry.

Tip the boxes over on one side and brush with glue and sprinkle with glitter. Do the same on the other side and on the top.

Ariel's tip:
Put your most treasured item at the top of your case, and show it off properly!

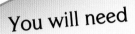

Snow White

Friendship Bands

We all know Snow White has seven best friends! Show your best friend how much you like them with this great friendship band in pretty princess colours.

You will need

♡ 4 strands of cotton thread: 2 mauve, 1 pink and 1 purple (or the colours of your choice), each 20 inches (50 cm) long
♡ 1 large bead
♡ 4 medium-sized beads

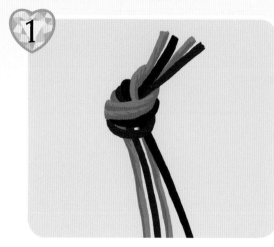

1 Take the 4 strands of cotton thread and knot them together, 8 inches (20cm) from one end.

2 Thread the large bead on the bracelet and push it up as far as the knot.

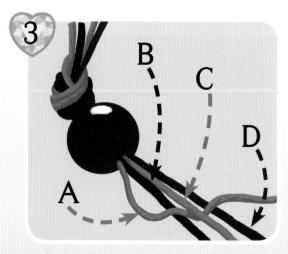

3 Spread out the 4 strands so that the 2 mauve strands are first and third from the left. Put A over B, under C and over D. Pull A gently to tighten the weave.

88

4

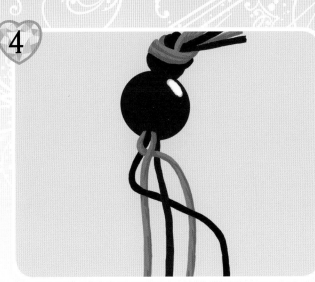

Continue weaving B over C, under D and over A, working over, under, over, under. Pull gently to tighten before starting on the next left-hand strand.

5

Continue weaving until you are about 3 inches (8cm) from the end, then tie the knotted strands into a knot, leaving the ends loose.

6

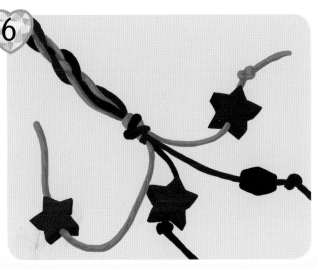

Thread a medium-sized bead onto each of the 4 loose strands and tie a knot to keep it in place.

Snow White's tip:
Give this band as a birthday present! Who would you give your band to?

Aurora Royal Crown

Aurora wears her royal crown with pride. This crown is fit for a royal princess! You can be the ruler of your own princess kingdom!

You will need

- 8 x 11 inch tracing paper and pencil
- Strip of gold cardboard 5 x 24 inches
- Scissors, white glue and brush
- Hologram film 1 x 24 inches
- 2 strips of gold cardboard: 1½ x 13 inches
- Paperclips and paper fastener
- Purple felt
- Dinner plate
- Cotton batting
- Black acrylic paint and fine brush
- Assorted coloured gems

1

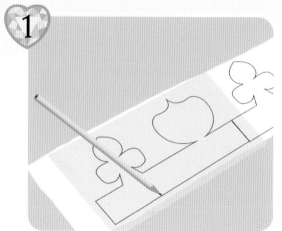

Draw the crown template. Transfer it onto the back of the gold cardboard, then repeat, putting the second section up to the first. Cut out the whole strip.

2

Glue the hologram film along the base, then glue gems along the top. Glue the two ends so the crown fits loosely on your head. Hold in place with paperclips. Let dry.

3

Push a paper fastener through where the strips meet.

Mark halfway between the shapes with the pencil. Glue the gold strips to the inside of the band where these marks are. Hold in place with paperclips. Let dry.

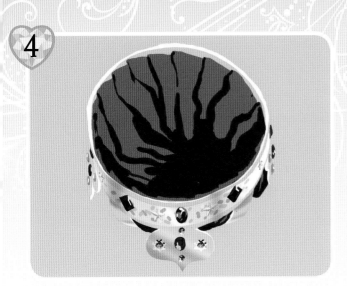

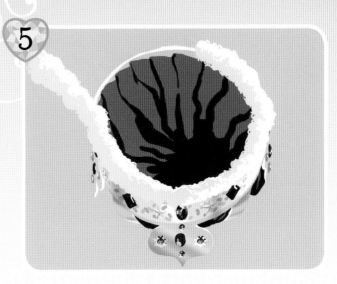

Trace around the dinner plate and cut out a circle of purple felt. Make small snips all around the outside of the felt circle. Glue the felt to the inner brim, gluing bit by bit along the clipped edge. Let dry.

Cut a strip of cotton batting about 2 inches (5cm) wide. Glue it along the bottom edge of the crown. Paint black spots about 1 inch (2.5cm) apart along the length of the cotton batting.

Aurora's tip:
Crown's are not only gold, but silver or pink, or any pretty colour you like!

Beautiful Fan

Jasmine loves living in such a hot place. But sometimes a Princess needs to cool down. This beautiful fan is perfect for hot weather or as a stylish accessory!

1

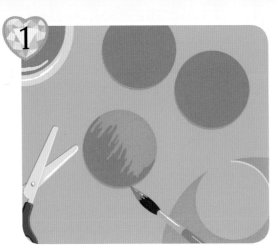

Draw three circles each 6 inches (15cm) in diameter on the cardboard. You could use a small plate as a guide. Cut out the circles. Paint in your favourite colours. Paint each side at a time allowing to dry.

You will need

- Thick cardboard
- Small plate
- Glue
- Pencil
- Paint
- 2 sticks
- Tape
- Ribbon
- Feathers
- Glitter glue

2

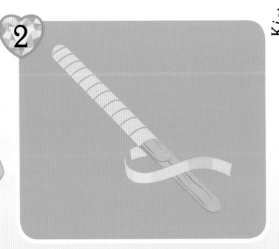

Tape two wooden sticks together, then wind some ribbon around the outside. Secure the ribbon ends in place with a dot of glue or tape.

Kids 3

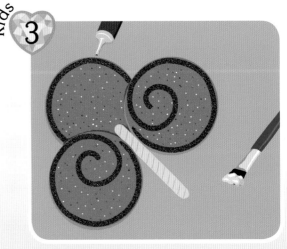

Glue the three circles together, arranging into a fan shape. Glue the stick into the middle. Using your glitter glue decorate the fan with a pretty pattern. Ensure this is left to dry.

Arrange feathers and gem on the fan. Glue feathers and gem to the fan when you are happy with the arrangement. Tie strips of ribbon to the bottom of the handle and stick another gem to the base where the ribbons join. Allow the glue to dry.

Tiana Celebration Mask

Tiana loves to wear a mask during Mardi Gras. You can make your own celebration mask for a special occasion or to put on your wall!

You will need

- Coloured card
- Pencil
- Feathers of mixed colours
- Sequins
- Scissors
- Glue
- Glitter glue
- Elastic

Fold a piece of 10 x 5 inches (25 x 12cm) card in half. Draw half a mask shape. Make the eye hole around 1 inch (3cm) from the folded edge. Cut out the mask outline and eye hole.

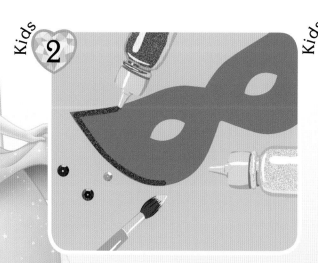

Decorate around the edge and eyes with glitter glue and allow to dry. Glue small sequins onto the mask to decorate. Leave to dry.

Turn the mask over and glue feathers along the top. Make sure they don't cover the eye holes. Allow to dry.

Tiana's tip:
You could make one of these for each of your friends, then take a picture of you all wearing them!

Make a small hole on each side of the mask. Thread a piece of elastic through each hole with a knot on the end. The knot should be tied on the reverse of the mask.

Cinderella Glitter Slippers

With help from the fairy godmother Cinderella sparkled at the royal ball in her slippers. Now you can too, with these pretty glitter slippers!

Kids 1

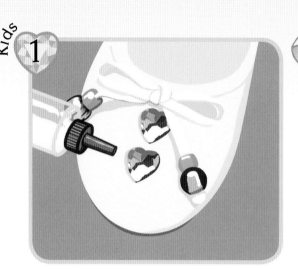

Glue the gems to the slipper and leave to dry.

You will need

- Pair of clean sneakers or canvas shoes
- Fabric paints
- Fabric pens
- Glitter
- Plastic gemstones
- Beads

Cinderella's tip:
You don't just have to try dots, you could draw flowers or hearts, or even write your name on your shoes!

Kids 2

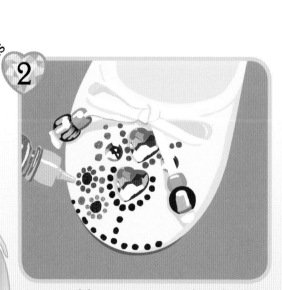

Next, add some more detail using the glitter glue. Gently make glittery dots on your shoes around the gems. Do one colour at a time and leave to dry before applying more.